AMARYLLIS

"HOW CAN I GO ON?"

Margaret Sammy

AMARYLLIS
"HOW CAN I GO ON?"

(poems)

Margaret Sammy

Margaret Sammy

Copyright ©2017 *Margaret Sammy*

ISBN: 978-978-54741-3-8

All rights reserved.
No part of this book may be reproduced, distributed, stored in a retrieval system or transmitted, in any form or by any means, electronic, electrostatic, magnetic tape, mechanical, photocopying, recording or otherwise without prior written permission from the Publisher.
For information about permission to reproduce selections from this book, write to info@wrr.ng
National Library of Nigeria Cataloguing-in-Publication Data

Printed and Published in Nigeria by:
Words Rhymes & Rhythm Limited
Suite C309, Global Plaza Plot 366, Obafemi Awolowo Way, Jabi District, Abuja, Nigeria.
08169027757, 08060109295
www.wrr.ng

Amaryllis

ACKNOWLEDGEMENT

I am tremendously grateful to God for the wisdom, grace, and enablement to write these poems.

My profound gratitude goes to my wonderful parents, Dr. & Mrs Victor Sammy, who support and make sure I am the best in all I do. I also want to express my heartfelt gratitude to my siblings Master David and Joseph Jovani Sammy who inspired me to write poems each day.

I extend my gratitude to my Pastor, Apostle King David Zilly Aggrey, and Lady Apostle Gladys Aggrey JP, who have spiritually mentored, motivated, and prayed for me to become who I am today.

This acknowledgement would not be complete without mentioning my grandmothers Mrs. Margaret Alameyeseigha and Mrs. Nene Beals, my patient and supportive literature teacher in my primary school (Vine International School) Mr. Robert Nabena and Mrs. Nina Jegede (founder & President, Vine International School), whose platform sharpened my intellect primarily and develop my writing skills. Thank you.

To the proprietress, management, staff and students of Green Oak International School, you are part of my success history.

Contents

ACKNOWLEDGEMENT 5
SMILES EACH DAY 8
HOW CAN I GO ON 9
MY CHOICE 10
HAPPINESS 11
HOLIDAY 12
MOTHER 13
FATHER 15
FAMILY 16
THE AFRICAN CHILD 17
LOVE 18
LEADERS AND RULERS 19
I PROMISE 20
WHY 21
UPON A STUDIOUS LANE 22
GOD 23
SET OUT 24
IF 25
A BORN STAR 26
IF I WERE ME 27
MY TEACHER'S SONG 28
THE GONG OF JUSTICE 29
MY REBIRTH 30
MY LEARNING CENTER 31
THE OLD POLICE MAN 32
WHEN FEAR SHUTS YOU IN 33
TRUE MEANING OF LIGHT 34
ONENESS 35
NO PLANS 36
WHY DO PEOPLE LIE 37
A WARRIOR'S HEARTBEAT 38
WHO BELLS THE CAT 39

THE LEOPARD AND THE WOLF 40
CHILDREN 41
LOVE LENS 42
HOW LONG WILL SPOKESMEN FORGET? 43
LOST LOVE CAN STILL BE FOUND 44
I SEEK CHANGE 45
MY QUESTION 46
MOTHER'S LOVE 47
TO MY MOM 48
THE FORGOTTEN SON (NIGER DELTA POEM)... 49
NIGERIA 50
AGATU MASSACRE 51
NOT WHAT WE SEEK 52
LIFE 53
NEVER BE ORDINARY 54
FROM A TINY ACORN TO A MIGHTY OAK 55
SOLEMN PRAYER 56
RESOLUTE 57
I AM CHIBOK 58
ABOUT THE AUTHOR 59

Margaret Sammy

SMILES EACH DAY

Smiles each day
What a pleasant sight

Smiles each day
It's not a mile away
Its free to everyone
It doesn't discriminate anyone
Both the rich and poor
Benefit from it

Smiles each day
My best costume
A simple smile lifts up one's face
Its free and neat
With no wrinkles and cracks
It makes frowning unlike you
It brings out your true color and beauty

Smiles each day
The best plastic surgery
You could give to yourself
The only item made for the natural beauty of everyone
To enjoy and be happy with
Smiles each day makes the world
A better place

HOW CAN I GO ON

How can I go on?
When the world is chasing me
A race I might never win
My legs fail me
I need help not encouragement
Why won't they listen to me?

I can't run anymore,
I am just a girl
Tomorrow's woman
I am out of breath
Can't you hear me?

I might be trapped in a box
With my talents strapped in my pouch
I plead for a moment to be heard
To be seen
Please don't say no!

If I do my part positively,
What about yours?
I am human
Not a machine
Listen to me
I beg to be heard

MY CHOICE

Life
A choice given to me
Make good use of it
You can be a doctor
A lawyer
An engineer
And so much more

Life
A choice given to me
They say when life gives you lemons
Make yourself lemonade
When life challenges you
See an opportunity to try harder

Some people are given life
Yet take it for granted
Make good use of yours

Life
A choice given to me
To leave a mark
To be my best
I'll make good use of mine
What's your choice in life?

HAPPINESS

Happiness,
What is this feeling in me?
Don't take it away
So pleasant,
So soothing,
Could it be joy?

Can it stay in me forever?
Maybe not so long
But long enough
To light me up
Light up my face
Ignite my eyes
And make me feel special all day long

Happiness the best song I can ever sing
The feeling of strength
That feeling I have saying I can fly
That feeling where I can do anything
The best names you can give to anyone

Happiness,
Can it be bought?
Can it be stolen?
Can it find?
What brings it?

Margaret Sammy

HOLIDAY

My time of rest and play
My worries are saved for another day

Holiday;
When I smell the daisies and roses a lot better than ever before
When the green grass is a sight to see

Holiday;
When family seems close
Closer than before
My sanctuary is made for rest.
The period were time is slower
If boring
But faster when fun

Holiday;
It's that time that no one has an excuse not to have some fun
That period when you feel so young
Younger than you have ever felt before

Holiday;
The worst time is when
It's coming to an end
It makes your work place feel like trouble
It makes school feel like prison
So special to so many people
And taken for granted by some people

Amaryllis

MOTHER

Mother;
My very own priceless jewel
A woman specially created for me
A woman specially created for me
With no regret what so ever

Mother;
My life giver
Heavens gift to me
The next thing anyone can and should adore after God
The person that is always so dear and special to me
Mother;
My nurse
Guide and teacher
Heavens treasure here on earth
Well done, my sweet mother.
My extra shoulder to lean on
The person I turn to
As a child in time of need
The only person that casts good spells
Just by the aroma of her food

Mother;
The sweeter kind of f
The person that risks it all
Just for me to be happy
The person that cools father down
So he would be gentle with me
And listen to my need

Mother;

Margaret Sammy

The person that wake up in the night
When I have only a cold to make sure
am better to the fullest of my strength
The person that sticks up for me
If no one will and makes me warm
That person that makes you worried
When she steps out of the house and is not back till night

Amaryllis

FATHER

Loving and caring
The strict part of life
Pushing me beyond limits
Always placing my need before his

Father,
Love so precious,
Kind and soothing
Lifting me up
Placing me on his cliff
To watch the waves crash on the shore
 The extra sale to the ship
The captain that stirs with peace, discipline and integrity
The first pillar to the house
And the door that knows the status of the family

The careful breadwinner
Watching and keeping track of all his steps
Making sure nothing affects me
Creating a level of security within his budget
To make sure I am always free and safe
From harm and fright
That shoulder strong enough to carry me

FAMILY

Family
Is it just father, mother, children and relatives?

Family
The foundation of human life

Family
There to help in time of need
Correct us when we go out of line.

Family
A child's first institution
Teaching us about what is ahead
Keeping us safe, snug and happy

Family
Teaching us charity,
Good character, respect and morals

Family
They push us to excellence,
Propel us to victory,
They see the future,
Long before we arrive

Family
Not just mother, father, children and relatives.
It's all these people and those there for you

Amaryllis

THE AFRICAN CHILD

Tomorrow's leaders
Never given a chance
Words fading away
Talents rotting within
Unused, never recognized, dormant

We remain resolute
In the face of daunting challenges
Burnt by harsh realities
We are tomorrow's leaders changing today

When everything else fails
We set sail
Determined to evolve
To help mold
To build our tomorrow today

Margaret Sammy

LOVE

Love
A grip so firm
Beauty to behold
Diverse meaning

Different strokes
For different folks
Deeper than feelings
Emotions and words

Love
Something I can't tell
Mother & child
Fireplace
A sight to behold

Love
Infant smile
A baby's first laugh
A sigh of relief

Love
Nature's gift to the world
A sign of divinity
A girl's first letter to her mom

Amaryllis

LEADERS AND RULERS

During tough times
Nations crumble
During tough times
Rules are broken

During tough times
Despair rules the land
Find me a place
Where all is well

Leaders against followers
Followers against leaders
Society is in turmoil
Find me a place
Where all is well

Margaret Sammy

I PROMISE

I promise to pay the debt
I promise to get your money
I'll go to school
I'll fly a kite
I'll do the dishes
I promise

I promise
I'll tell no one you told me
I promise not to tell
Say no more
I forgive you

A promise
Never fulfilled
Never kept
Bummer! Bummer!
Make a promise you can keep

Amaryllis

WHY

Why do people die?
Only for tears to roll
Why do seeds die?
To sprout again

Why do babies cry?
Only to smile through a mother's cuddle

Why do rulers lie?
And leaders fight wars?

Why is Africa blessed?
Yet struggle with hunger and aids?
In one world of freedom

Why do people feel they are better than others?
We are of the same flesh and blood
Taken and seen as one
We stand strong united
But fall when divided

Why make yourself feel greater and more superior
when you can't live alone
And can never tell what the future holds

Why can't I be me?
And nobody has to look down on anybody

Margaret Sammy

UPON A STUDIOUS LANE

Upon a studious lane
I'll walk
The prize for years to come
I'll win

I love the smell of writing sheet
Too harsh to bear
When homework calls

Alert To hear my teachers speak
Upon this studious lane
I'll walk

Amaryllis

GOD

God my unchangeable
Dependable, reliable friend
And guide.

God, giver of anything
And everything I ask for my betterment

God never gives up on me
Not for any reason
He is exceedingly
Abundantly above all I ask, think or ever imagine
His love is everlasting
Stretching farther than my eyes can see

God sees my end from my beginning
Knows how I feel even before I feel low Happy or scared

God fights my enemies at any time
And is able to bring them down
Making sure they never rise again
I breathe Oxygen freely from Him.

God uses ordinary people, lighten up the extra within them and they become extraordinary

How can I describe you? God

Margaret Sammy

SET OUT

I solved your problem
But I can't seem to help myself
I was part of your yesterday
But I can't do everything,

Or be everything…
But I must be something,
Something I must discover
Something I won't fear
I must be me.

I asked for help but they didn't listen
They thought I wouldn't succeed
But see me now they are pleading
Asking me how did I make it
All I can say is GOD

IF

If I were a bird
I'll soar high above all lush green valleys
Looking down at human problems
Like dotted grains spread across a field

If I had a wishing wand,
I'll stretch it far across lush green fields
Providing solutions to every problem known to man

If I were a star
I'll give wishes to those who work hard

If I were an adult
I'll stand in line to vote
To build my country
I'll be a patriot

Margaret Sammy

A BORN STAR

A born star,
To row in troubled waters
A born star,
The right of every girl in my hand
To protect,
To shield,

Ready for danger, trouble and war
To speak volumes for my cause
To show bravery, courage and boldness
Waiting for the day to come
A day when every girl will matter

Their rights protected
Free from abuse
Free from tradition
And the shackles of the prowler

Roll out your drums you women
Young and wrinkled
Free and speckled
Play the beats of a revolution
I am that star.

Amaryllis

IF I WERE ME

If I were me,
Self-thinking wouldn't be hindered in uniforms,
Adulthood, my book to be opened at my pace,
Life my road to walk, one step at a time

If I were me,
I'll chart my course,
Pick my battles,
Guard my ears,
And choose what I see,
Saving myself to be me.

If I were me
My taste for adventure will never remain the same
The love for irrelevant things could fade
Touch lives positively as I want
Be how I want

Without been judged
Have my feel of been a girl
Be excited, full of smiles and adventurous
For my future is now
And I have to be me

Margaret Sammy

MY TEACHER'S SONG

I heard my teacher sing
Of a lion's fame
I like to hear the frightening roar
Of a lion's call
The terrible scare, of a lions loud rumbling
The thunderous roar, of the jungles pride
Songs about a lion's tail, big head
And its small waist

Its head stands for its level of pride
How huge it is with its mane
Symbols of its strength
As the king of the jungle
Its tail a very special feature
With an extraordinary style
Showing the heirs to come and how fragile they are, at enfant
But flawless they would be when it's their turn to rule
Its small waist epitomizing its patience
He is at first patient, once hungry. When he can't find any good meat, the hunger runs down to his waist. He gets angry; with that anger it goes to hunt before the hunger runs down to its legs

My teacher's song,
My guard to life with time, chance and opportunities
that yields advancement, achievement and abundance

THE GONG OF JUSTICE

Listen
To Its beat
Controls the heart beat
Only the guilty hearts beat faster
No one can ever outsmart the gong of justice

Listen
Its beat awakens the guilty
Makes them confess
It is the great instrument of victory
For those whose sleep are stolen

Look
The two sides of the gong of justice
It congratulates
It holds bound
And ushers in a new dawn
It brings both the guilty
And the innocent
Before the jury
Long lives the gong of justice

Margaret Sammy

MY REBIRTH

My name is soon to be told
For all humanity to know
You look at me with no hope in sight
Unknown to you, I'm the greatest of all

My egg is about to hatch
I announce the time for my rebirth
I'll bring my fragrance along
With my pen in hand
And a scribble pad to write
I come to you in a strange way
Strange to those who can't comprehend
With a purpose seen only by people who support me
Understood by people who love me
And adored by people who honor me
They are patient and reading until my day of rebirth comes
Hoping as I go far all in my way will be success

My egg is hatching
My talents have been completely soaked up in me
No one knows how I would look
When I would grow
How I would shine forth
My rebirth has come
with the dawn of a new era

MY LEARNING CENTER

This home is filled with great promises and goals
A home were dreams come true
A home with love, peace, joy, and acceptance

This is no ordinary home
Could you guess this home?
Most people hate it
Make mockery of it
Some dread it

A home filled with good morals
Where all your wishes are fulfilled
Yet you refuse to come here
To be part of this great opportunity
A great opportunity to strive for excellence, achievement and victory

This home should never be missed
This home is nothing but a 'great school
With an atmosphere always filled with success

Margaret Sammy

THE OLD POLICE MAN

Never absent
Always combat ready
He is big
Tough, rough and true
His polished shoes
And silver buttons make him proud

Left, right
Left, right
Chest out
Arm swinging
He moves along with his riffle

Intimidating night owls
With his biceps
Holding his head high
He strolls along
The tough old policeman
Tough, rough and true
His silver buttons makes him so proud
His over polished shoe making him feel so proud
And accomplishing His orders given out makes him feel powerful

Amaryllis

WHEN FEAR SHUTS YOU IN

When idleness covers
There is still a chance for good
You can still find a way out

Why give up
When you haven't even tried
You call for help
But help is within

You blame the government
But the government won't hear
You blame corruption
Yet hail corruption

Suddenly you conclude a spell
Or a curse is over you
Seeking for hands to be laid on you

Why lie to yourselves
How long will fear and idleness shut you in?
Why wait for help
When you can help

Margaret Sammy

TRUE MEANING OF LIGHT

Light
With the twinkle of an eye
Light
Comes like a strike of pain
Light
Covers any dark secret
Light
Far away from harm
Light
Brings life to any thing
Light
A little spell of wonder
Light
My first gift to all
Light
My first sight at birth
Light
My special gift

Light
My ordinary spot to shine

ONENESS

Friendship
A bond of togetherness
Friendship
A scent of love and oneness
Friendship
Three Musketeers as one
Friendship
All for one and one for all
Friendship
A simple spark that signifies peace
Friendship
More beautiful than fireworks

Friendship
A bond of love
Beauty to behold

Friendship
A feeling of completeness

Friendship
A person in time of need
Friendship;
When true, doesn't fade away
Friendship;
The people that make you feel awesome

Margaret Sammy

NO PLANS

An action not deeply thought
An element with no purpose at all
A random attitude with no sense of honour
A plan to fail

A business plan with no money to invest
A school without a single teacher
A hospital without even one doctor

All said
Can be said in another
If you fail to plan
You have planned to fail

Set a good plan and watch the way things will fall in place
Why most leaders fail a times
Thinking the problem are the people
But actually there is no plan or plans
For the betterment of the nation

All things will have purpose
No opportunity will be taken for granted
Every moment will always teach you a good lesson
Every action will turn out for the best

But! What is a good plan without Action?
No plans

Amaryllis

WHY DO PEOPLE LIE

Why do people lie to cover up their guilt?
To make a fool out of others or themselves
To make a point that is pointless
To remove the shame that knocks on their door that can be seen

To keep a tradition as foolish as ever
To protect the things that should be broken

Why do people lie?
Why do they seek to destroy truth?

   Why do people lie to love?
When love is the greatest gift of all
The fact of living together in harmony
Shattered by the little fake word that spills out from your mouth

Why do people lie?
Why make faults impressions
But we are all the same
Forgetting everyone has a specific purpose

Margaret Sammy

A WARRIOR'S HEARTBEAT

My father told me
The tale of a warrior
He sang to me
The tune of a warrior's heart beat

He wakes up with his gaze fixed to heaven
And a heart soaked in God
He told me of his passion
He never had a double life
He could give his all to the needy
And strive to see peace enthroned

My father told me
He shared with me
The tale of a warrior
He sang to me
The tune of a warrior's heart beat

WHO BELLS THE CAT

During tough times
Nations crumble
During tough times
Laws are broken

The people must survive,
We don't care who gets hurt
Treasures are looted
Criminality becomes a way of life
Rules are made,
But they are meant to be broken

Rulers against followers
Followers armed against rulers
Despair rules the land
Blood shot eyes on the prowl
Who will bell the cat?
No mouse in sight yet

Margaret Sammy

THE LEOPARD AND THE WOLF

It's about that time
Season fast changing
The clock ticks towards the ballot
All these processes someone has passed

They come to you
Clothed in sheepskin
They act as though they have changed their spots
Can the leopard change its spots?
Never have I seen a wolf half sheep, half human
They preach love
Only to lure the masses
There is no love in their heart
They preach change
Only for their pockets
They seek to remain
To continue in their ways

It's about that time
Season fast changing
When fathers will stand in line
To choose a cage

Amaryllis

CHILDREN

The unproductive
Yet excessively expensive

Children;
The most vulnerable
Yet overly protected

Children;
The loudest fragments
Yet hushed, silenced in prime

Children;
The most controlled
Yet controlling and dominating

Children;
Shouted at even when they are doing there very best
Taken for granted almost all the time
People using them to form a story not so true
Yet the future's hope and dream

Children;
Whose contributions are neglected todays
Yet are tomorrow's inventors

Margaret Sammy

LOVE LENS

When I have ceased to break my wings
Against the faultiness of things
And learned that compromises
Wait behind each hardly opened gate

Not disregarding the countenance of each
Nor the independence of one's choice

I come of age
Devoid of judgmental caprice
And I cease to see myself as right
When the choice of others do not agree with mine

It is easier to ridicule ones choice
To grow my one sided affection
Of the things I choose
That doth seem right

But I come of age
When I see me in others
And others through my love lens
When I indeed learn to break my wings
Against the faultiness of things
Things unclear to me
But faultless to others
Far be it that I fall prey
To the judgmental caprice of another
Of the things I deem faultless

Amaryllis

HOW LONG WILL SPOKESMEN FORGET?

How long will we be at each other's throat?
How long will our spokesmen forget?
Are we forgetful of events of the past?
How be it that we then call for war
In time of peace
Beat the drum of disaffection
At dinner time

How long will our spokesmen forget?
How long will they forget the true meaning
Of oneness
Of togetherness
And friendship

How long will my countrymen remain impoverished?
Shattered always by men who seek to grow
Their own belly
Will they not call for equity?
I am tired of this playfulness
Are we not ashamed of what we've become?
How long shall we be at this?
Shall we sit and watch
While our bellies become flattened

Margaret Sammy

LOST LOVE CAN STILL BE FOUND

Love
Something people lose
To find again

Love
It is easily lost
And easily found
How?
You may ask
Look in your heart
Go by your guts
And you will find your
Reasonable answer

Today is a new day
See John
See Lola
They are happy together
Love found for a lifetime.
Happy couple;

See Josh and Mary
Their honey moon is almost over
And they lost their love for each other
So sad
They once loved each other
Love lost, never found again
Unknown to them
Love can easily be found

I SEEK CHANGE

This change has brought with it
Distrust
Communal clashes
And acrimony among siblings
This change is far from change
Show me change

The real change
The kind I seek
The kind we need
From bad to good
Not bad to worse

I seek change
To grow
To be better
The type where I'll become
A model for all

Margaret Sammy

MY QUESTION

Our roads are bad
Our educational system in shambles
With no electricity
I have to rely on my lamp
To make my pap

Our elites have to travel abroad
For quality health care
Because our doctors are on strike

Then I remember the routine speeches
The promise of a new Nigeria
When will it come?
I don't know....

But first I need food on my table
Good water to drink...
Peace's to enable me play and think
Jobs to engage kidnappers
Healthy environment to reduce hunger

When will all these troubles
Seize to exist
And become tales of the past?

Amaryllis

MOTHER'S LOVE

The stare you get
That tells it all
The gentle voice
That spews reason
The warm embrace
That keeps you warm

Carrying herself unselfishly
She holds you close
Away from harm
Waters you
So you can grow

Her pretty smile
Lights up the room
She taught you
What a girl should be.

Making sure your dressed to match the occasion
Reminding you of the fierce world outside the compound
Reminding you your always beautiful
When you fall and get messed up
Not leaving you all alone for you to hustle by yourself

Margaret Sammy

TO MY MOM

Thank you
For being a friend so dear

Thank you
For being a shoulder so near

Thank you
For giving a smile so dear
Your tender voice
To guide my way

Thank you
For been there when I had no one,
For not allowing me to go on the street
Never letting me suffer one bit

Thank you
For telling me the truth
When I needed it
For your advice and lectures is life in deed

Thank you for all you have done
Thank you for being my Mom

Amaryllis

THE FORGOTTEN SON (NIGER DELTA POEM)

He woke up that morning
With a yawn
Probably hungry
From the humble creeks of the Delta

With no one to care,
Mother died of a strange illness,
Father is nowhere near.
Treated like an outcast
His eyes filled with sadness,
Blood shot and sunken
He's the forgotten son
He wanders on his own

A son that lives in a creeks full of dollars; yet no food to eat

A young man that lives in the swamps of the Delta and yet no clean water to drink. He must be the forgotten creek boy who once holds the nation on ransom.

Wait! He heard the sounds of a crowd gathering
Its Amnesty they said.
A breath of hope! He seems

Margaret Sammy

NIGERIA

Nigeria
Oh my Nigeria
Great nation
Great people
Beautiful beyond description

We are bold
We are industrious
We are the future
That we hope for
Let us come together

Sheath your swords,
Let's build together.
The future of our land
Rests on our shoulders
Let us all give a helping hand

Not to flee in time of trouble
Not to forget what brotherly love has enable others to build

Amaryllis

AGATU MASSACRE

Our elders, are you no more our mentors
alive? Are your tales and guidance no more
lights on our paths? And are we (the youths)
no more tomorrow's leaders?

Why do you remain silent?
When they enthrone evil
Why do you look the other way?
When they steal our sleep

Arise! Old man,
Call these masquerades to order
Put an end to this madness
We ask to sleep
With our eyes closed

We believe that God will answer our
prayers. But, we also know that we have to
ask God first before He answers.
So, our hopes are in God.

If we change our ways, pray, believe in our
Great GOD to grand our prayers. God will.
Therefore arise and keep on rising.

Margaret Sammy

NOT WHAT WE SEEK

Lost in a well of desire
Seeking for a recall of dignity and glory
A dark giant
On a divinely ordained throne of greatness
A redefinition of values

Still lost at the altar of corruption
With our desired rebirth
Blaming corruption

Enthroning faithful brave hearts
On the destructive pile of tribalism
Hiding behind the monster of religion
Draped in robes of honesty and duty

LIFE

Is Life in its real sense a School?
The world our classroom
Circumstances our teacher

When do we graduate?
Who marks the scorecard?
Who owns the school?

Whether sick
Tired or worn out
There is no excuse
For a little laxity

You get a lash
On your bare buttocks
From a stern disciplinarian
In all, no excuses
We sit still
As we wait for the final bell

Time....

Margaret Sammy

NEVER BE ORDINARY

Never be ordinary
The beauty in you
Always makes you extra ordinary
But people don't know where to find it
Many may doubt you or even themselves

But listen
You are the pilot of your dreams,
Look for your landing
Before it's too late

Never be ordinary
Be yourself
Always find a way across, around and
Over a situation
Find your inner warrior
Try, try, and never give up

Always be the better version of yourself
Never try to be ordinary
And follow someone with an extra ordinary gift
To help boost yours
Find your style
Look for what fits you best
Try to be the best you can ever be
Always look for the solution to the problem
Don't complain about the problem.
Never be ordinary

Amaryllis

FROM A TINY ACORN TO A MIGHTY OAK

From the giant
Fails the tiny egg cup
Disadvantaged by size
Buried by nature
Nursed by the rain

It fights through
With strength
Endurance
And dependability
In time
A fallen egg cup
Becomes an elevated giant

Ready to bring the freshest fruit
from its large trunk
Ready to be a shade to lives
that will nurture or bruise it
Ready and happy to have a major job
That will help in the breathing of nature

Margaret Sammy

SOLEMN PRAYER

May we keep the peace
While we await justice
May we learn to respect each other
Not endure each other

May we love our own
Even if they fall short
May we keep our guns at home
When we approach the table of dialogue
May we learn that actions speak louder than words

That people have different reactions to occasions
May we learn that not everyone is to be tossed around
with disrespect

May we learn to be our brother's keeper
And not our brother's slayer
May we learn to give a helping hand to all those in
need
Not to turn your face away from them
And ignore the cry of the poor
May we learn to be helpful in always

Amaryllis

RESOLUTE

Whether they know it or not
Whether they like it or not
Whether directly or indirectly
Willingly or unwillingly

We must change someday
Illegitimate will become legitimate
Corruption will become incorruptible
We shall go to bed with our doors open
Walk around brandishing our wallets

Sons will look at their fathers
They shall be proud at the legacies left
Men will look into their wallets
Without been scared of the amount inside
Till all comes to an end
We look to GOD for help

We must change the way we waste items
We must change the way we see occasions
There is absolutely no difference between the white man and the black man
The only difference is our mind, mentality, and ways of thinking
Change
Whether sweet or noted

I AM CHIBOK

Their souls speak to us
Dead or alive
They'll haunt us one day
We must look inward
Decide for ourselves
To protect what is left
Even as we search for the lost

Shall we all sit idle?
Glorying in our past
While we are haunted by the present
Why hold a girl ransom
When she bears the seed for tomorrow
Have you no conscience?

Do we dance today away?
Or remain silent
As the numbers and days pile up

Do we arm ourselves in readiness?
Or quibble over semantics
When our houses are blazed
And rifles deafen our ears

I am Chibok
I speak from the distance
In readiness as the havoc unfolds
I lay in wait for the herdsman's riffle shot

Amaryllis

ABOUT THE AUTHOR

Margaret Sammy was born in 2004. She began writing poems at the age of 10 and was greatly influenced by her teacher. She draws her inspiration from observing the Nigerian society and seeks to lend her voice towards child education, societal morals and peace in societies.

Margaret's work depicts a girl's will to write. Her devotion to poetry has yielded "Amaryllis" her first collection of poems.

Margaret is an eighth grade pupil of Green Oak International School, Port Harcourt.

AMARYLLIS is her first published work.

www.ingramcontent.com/pod-product-compliance
Lightning Source LLC
Chambersburg PA
CBHW032058040426
42449CB00007B/1131